POETICAL SKETCHES

By WILLIAM BLAKE

TABLE OF CONTENTS

THE period between 1768 and 1783 may be described as one of utter stagnation in poetry—the low-water mark of the eighteenth century, in no part of it very fruitful in verse of a high order. With Mason, Hayley, and Darwin installed as the high priests of the Muses, and a host of satellites of the Charlotte Smith and Jerningham order, pouring forth volumes of mediocre verses, tolerable now neither to gods nor men nor columns—feeble echoes of a school which, at its best, drew but little of its inspiration from Nature, how welcome to the ear are the fresh notes of William Blake, recalling here the grand Elizabethan melodies, anticipating now the pathos and simplicity of Wordsworth, now the subtlety and daring of Shelley.

The "Poetical Sketches," though not printed till 1783, a year after Cowper's first volume made its appearance, were written, it appears, between 1768 and 1777—the earliest in the author's twelfth and the latest in his twentieth year. They lay in manuscript for six years, before, by the good offices of Flaxman and other friends, they could get into print. The little volume, which extended to only seventy pages, cannot, indeed, be said to have been published. The whole impression seems to have fallen into the hands of Blake's personal friends: certain it is that it attracted no notice whatever from the critics. The book has now become so scarce that no copy is to be found even in the British Museum; and as Mr. Rossetti has confined himself to a few selections, we have thought that a faithful reprint of the whole from a copy that has luckily fallen into our hands, might be an acceptable present to the numerous body of readers now awakening gradually to a sense of the rare merit and originality of the artist-poet, and form a fitting companion volume to the "Songs of Innocence and Experience."

Before closing the bibliographical portion of our remarks, we must say a final word respecting the principle adopted by Mr. Rossetti in his reprint of some of these poems in the second volume of Gilchrist's "Life of Blake." Once for all, while rendering due homage to his genius and rare critical perception, as well as to the great services he has rendered to the fame of Blake, we must firmly protest against the dangerous precedent he has established of tampering with his author's text. Much ruggedness of metre and crudeness of expression he has doubtless removed or toned down by this process : but, however delicately and tastefully done, we contend that the doing of it was unwarrantable—nay, that it destroys to a certain extent the historical value of the poems. It was the growth of this mischievous system which prevented the readers of the eighteenth century from enjoying a pure text of Shakespeare ; which to this day, in nine editions out of ten, gives us a corrupt and mutilated text of such writers as Bunyan, Walton, and De Foe, and which has spoilt some of the finest hymns in our language. For where is the process, once admitted as legitimate, to stop? It is not every emendator who possesses the taste and judgment of Mr. Rossetti, and, in a case like the present one, where the original edition is almost inaccessible as a check, what protection has the reader against the caprice or vanity of an editor who does not adhere religiously to his author's text? Mr. Rossetti (though sanctioned by Mr. Swinburne) has no more right to alter William Blake's poems than Mr. Millais would have to paint out some obnoxious detail of medievalism in a work of Giotto or Cimabue; or Mr. Leighton to improve some flaw in the flesh-colour of Correggio. The duty of an editor, in such a case as that of Blake's "Poetical Sketches," is confined to the silent correction of obvious clerical errors, and to the rectification of faulty orthography or punctuation, due either to the lax and uncertain spelling of the time, or to the ignorance and carelessness of the printer.

Having spoken this word in season, we pass on to the pleasanter duty of examining these poems separately.

Of the opening poems addressed to the four Seasons, we may say that the first three, though marred here and there by irregularities of metre, have a wealth of imagery and felicity of expression worthy of some of the finest things in Keats and Shelley and Tennyson.[1] There are lines too in them which stand out rememberable for ever, and haunt the ear with their melody. The "Winter," though it opens vigorously, soon falls into the pseudo-Ossianic grandiloquence, of which there is also a taint in several other pieces, and the last three lines, stumbling and staggering, remind us irresistibly of the same incongruous blending of sublime and ludicrous images (going on halting feet) in Turner's unfortunate "Fallacies of Hope."

The lines to the "Evening Star" are almost Tennysonian in happily-chosen epithet and perfect cadence of music:

"Smile on our loves; and while thou drawest the
"Blue curtains of the sky, scatter thy silver dew
"On every flower that shuts its sweet eyes
"In timely sleep. Let thy west wind sleep on
"The lake; speak silence with thy glimmering eyes,
"And wash the dusk with silver."
"Fair Eleanor"—a sort of blank-verse ballad of the Radcliffe type of crime and mystery and horror—is a somewhat abortive attempt, much in the style of some of Shelley's early poetry of the St. Irvyne and Margaret Nicholson period—not without lines of singular beauty that stand out in relief to the dulness and insipidity of the rest.

But what fitting tribute can we pay to the marvellous beauty of the six lyrics which follow, and of the lines "To the Muses?" We must go back to apology for the less happy efforts of a poet who in his best things has hardly fallen short of the large utterance of the Elizabethan dramatists, the pastoral simplicity of Wordsworth, the subtlety and fire of Shelley, and the lyrical tenderness of Tennyson.

TO SPRING.

Poetical sketches reprint 23 (initial).png THOU with dewy locks, who lookest
down
Thro' the clear windows of the morning,
 turn

Thine angel eyes upon our western isle,
Which in full choir hails thy approach, O Spring!

The hills tell each other, and the listening
Valleys hear; all our longing eyes are turn'd
Up to thy bright pavilions: issue forth,
And let thy holy feet visit our clime.
Come o'er the eastern hills, and let our winds
Kiss thy perfumed garments; let us taste
Thy morn and evening breath; scatter thy pearls
Upon our lovesick land that mourns for thee.

O deck her forth with thy fair fingers; pour
Thy soft kisses on her bosom; and put
Thy golden crown upon her languish'd head,
Whose modest tresses were bound up for thee!

TO SUMMER.

O THOU who passest thro' our valleys in
 Thy strength, curb thy fierce steeds, allay the
 heat
That flames from their large nostrils! thou, O Summer,
Oft pitchedst here thy golden tent, and oft
Beneath our oaks hast slept, while we beheld
With joy, thy ruddy limbs and flourishing hair.

Beneath our thickest shades we oft have heard
Thy voice, when noon upon his fervid car
Rode o'er the deep of heaven: beside our springs
Sit down, and in our mossy valleys, on
Some bank beside a river clear, throw thy
Silk draperies off, and rush into the stream:
Our valleys love the Summer in his pride.

Our bards are famed who strike the silver wire:
Our youth are bolder than the southern swains:
Our maidens fairer in the sprightly dance:
We lack not songs, nor instruments of joy,
Nor echoes sweet, nor waters clear as heaven,
Nor laurel wreaths against the sultry heat.

TO AUTUMN.

O AUTUMN, laden with fruit, and stain'd
 With the blood of the grape, pass not, but sit
Beneath my shady roof, there thou mayst rest,
And tune thy jolly voice to my fresh pipe,
And all the daughters of the year shall dance!
Sing now the lusty song of fruits and flowers.

"The narrow bud opens her beauties to
"The sun, and love runs in her thrilling veins;
"Blossoms hang round the brows of morning, and
"Flourish down the bright check of modest eve,
"Till clustering Summer breaks forth into singing,
"And feather'd clouds strew flowers round her head.

"The spirits of the air live on the smells
"Of fruit; and joy, with pinions light, roves round
"The gardens, or sits singing in the trees."
Thus sang the jolly Autumn as he sat;
Then rose, girded himself, and o'er the bleak
Hills fled from our sight; but left his golden load.

TO WINTER.

O WINTER! bar thine adamantine doors:
The north is thine; there hast thou built thy dark
Deep-founded habitation. Shake not thy roofs
Nor bend thy pillars with thine iron car.

He hears me not, but o'er the yawning deep
Rides heavy; his storms are unchain'd, sheathed
In ribbed steel; I dare not lift mine eyes;
For he hath rear'd his sceptre o'er the world.

Lo! now the direful monster, whose skin clings
To his strong bones, strides o'er the groaning rocks:
He withers all in silence, and in his hand
Unclothes the earth, and freezes up frail life.

He takes his seat upon the cliffs, the mariner
Cries in vain. Poor little wretch! that deal'st
With storms, till heaven smiles, and the monster
Is driven yelling to his caves beneath Mount Hecla.

4

TO THE EVENING STAR.

THOU fair-hair'd angel of the evening,
Now, whilst the sun rests on the mountains, light
Thy bright torch of love—thy radiant crown
Put on, and smile upon our evening bed!
Smile on our loves; and, while thou drawest the
Blue curtains of the sky, scatter thy silver dew
On every flower that shuts its sweet eyes
In timely sleep. Let thy west wind sleep on
The lake; speak silence with thy glimmering eyes,
And wash the dusk with silver. Soon, full soon,
Dost thou withdraw; then the wolf rages wide,
And the lion glares thro' the dun forest:
The fleeces of our flocks are cover'd with
Thy sacred dew: protect them with thine influence.

TO MORNING.

O HOLY virgin! clad in purest white,
Unlock heaven's golden gates and issue forth;
Awake the dawn that sleeps in heaven; let light
Rise from the chambers of the east, and bring
The honey'd dew that cometh on waking day.
O radiant morning, salute the sun,
Roused like a huntsman to the chase, and with
Thy buskin'd feet appear upon our hills.

FAIR ELEANOR.

THE bell struck one and shook the silent tower;
The graves give up their dead: fair Eleanor
Walk'd by the castle-gate, and looked in:
A hollow groan ran thro' the dreary vaults.

She shriek'd aloud, and sunk upon the steps,
On the cold stone her pale cheek. Sickly smells
Of death, issue as from a sepulchre,
And all is silent but the sighing vaults.

Chill death withdraws his hand, and she revives;
Amazed she finds herself upon her feet,
And, like a ghost, thro' narrow passages
Walking, feeling the cold walls with her hands.

Fancy returns, and now she thinks of bones
And grinning skulls, and corruptible death
Wrapt in his shroud; and now fancies she hears
Deep sighs, and sees pale sickly ghosts gliding.
At length, no fancy, but reality
Distracts her. A rushing sound, and the feet
Of one that fled, approaches.—Ellen stood,
Like a dumb statue, froze to stone with fear.

The wretch approaches, crying, "The deed is done;
"Take this, and send it by whom thou wilt send;
"It is my life—send it to Eleanor:—
"He's dead, and howling after me for blood!

"Take this," he cried; and thrust into her arms
A wet napkin, wrapt about; then rush'd
Past, howling: she received into her arms
Pale death, and follow'd on the wings of fear.

They pass'd swift thro' the outer gate; the wretch,
Howling, leap'd o'er the wall into the moat,
Stifling in mud. Fair Ellen pass'd the bridge,
And heard a gloomy voice cry, "Is it done?"

As the deer wounded Ellen flew over
The pathless plain; as the arrows that fly
By night; destruction flies, and strikes in darkness.
She fled from fear, till at her house arrived.
Her maids await her; on her bed she falls,
That bed of joy where erst her lord hath press'd:
" Ah, woman's fear! " she cried, " Ah, cursed duke!
" Ah, my dear lord! ah, wretched Eleanor!

" My lord was like a flower upon the brows
" Of lusty May! Ah, life as frail as flower!
" O ghastly death! withdraw thy cruel hand,
" Seek'st thou that flower to deck thy horrid temples?

" My lord was like a star in highest heaven

7

" Drawn down to earth by spells and wickedness;
" My lord was like the opening eyes of day,
" When western winds creep softly o'er the flowers.

" But he is darken'd; like the summer's noon
" Clouded; fall'n like the stately tree, cut down;
" The breath of heaven dwelt among his leaves.
" O Eleanor, weak woman, fill'd with woe!"

Thus having spoke, she raised up her head,
And saw the bloody napkin by her side,
Which in her arms she brought; and how, tenfold
More terrified, saw it unfold itself.
Her eyes were fix'd; the bloody cloth unfolds,
Disclosing to her sight the murder'd head
Of her dear lord, all ghastly pale, clotted
With gory blood; it groan'd, and thus it spake:

"O Eleanor, behold thy husband's head
"Who, sleeping on the stones of yonder tower,
"Was 'reft of life by the accursed duke!
"A hired villain turn'd my sleep to death!

"O Eleanor, beware the cursed duke,
"O give not him thy hand, now I am dead;
"He seeks thy love; who, coward, in the night,
"Hired a villain to bereave my life."

She sat with dead cold limbs, stiflen'd to stone;
She took the gory head up in her arms;
She kiss'd the pale lips; she had no tears to shed;
She hugg'd it to her breast, and groan'd her last.

SONG.

HOW sweet I roam'd from field to field
And tasted all the summer's pride,
Till I the Prince of Love beheld
Who in the sunny beams did glide.

He shew'd me lilies for my hair,
And blushing roses for my brow;
He led me thro' his gardens fair
Where all his golden pleasures grow.

With sweet May-dews my wings were wet,
And Phœbus fired my vocal rage;
He caught me in his silken net,
And shut me in his golden cage.

He loves to sit and hear me sing,
Then, laughing, sports and plays with me;
Then stretches out my golden wing
And mocks my loss of liberty.

SONG.

MY silks and fine array,
My smiles and languish'd air
By love are driven away;
And mournful lean Despair
Brings me yew to deck my grave:
Such end true lovers have.

His face is fair as heaven
When springing buds unfold;
O why to him was't given,
Whose heart is wintry cold?
His breast is love's all-worshipp'd tomb,
Where all love's pilgrims come.

Bring me an axe and spade,
Bring me a winding sheet;
When I my grave have made
Let winds and tempests beat:
Then down I'll lie, as cold as clay.
True love doth pass away!

SONG.

LOVE and harmony combine
And around our souls entwine,
While thy branches mix with mine
And our roots together join.

Joys upon our branches sit
Chirping loud and singing sweet;
Like gentle streams beneath our feet
Innocence and virtue meet.

Thou the golden fruit dost bear,
I am clad in flowers fair;
Thy sweet boughs perfume the air,
And the turtle buildeth there.

There she sits and feeds her young,
Sweet I hear her mournful song;
And thy lovely leaves among
There is love; I hear his tongue.

There his charming nest doth lay,
There he sleeps the night away;
There he sports along the day
And doth among our branches play.

SONG.

I LOVE the jocund dance,
The softly-breathing song,
Where innocent eyes do glance
And where lisps the maiden's tongue.

I love the laughing vale,
I love the echoing hill,
Where mirth does never fail,
And the jolly swain laughs his fill.

I love the pleasant cot,
I love the innocent bower,
Where white and brown is our lot
Or fruit in the mid-day hour.

I love the oaken seat,
Beneath the oaken tree,
Where all the old villagers meet,
And laugh our sports to see.

I love our neighbours all,
But, Kitty, I better love thee;
And love them I ever shall,
But thou art all to me.
SONG.

MEMORY, hither come
And tune your merry notes:
And while upon the wind
Your music floats
I'll pore upon the stream
Where sighing lovers dream,
And fish for fancies as they pass
Within the watery glass.

I'll drink of the clear stream
And hear the linnet's song,
And there I'll lie and dream
The day along:
And, when night comes, I'll go
To places fit for woe
Walking along the darken'd valley
With silent Melancholy.[1]

1. Can we trace in the opening lines of Tennyson's Sonnet, published in The Englishman's Magazine, in August, 1831, an unintentional echo of the melody of the last two lines, or is it merely one of those accidental coincidences not uncommon among great poets? Ed.

MAD SONG.

THE wild winds weep,
  And the night is a-cold;
Come hither, Sleep,
  And my griefs enfold:
But lo! the morning peeps
Over the eastern steeps,
And the rustling beds of dawn
The earth do scorn.

Lo! to the vault
  Of paved heaven,
With sorrow fraught
  My notes are driven:
They strike the ear of night,
  Make weep the eyes of day;
They make mad the roaring winds,
  And with tempests play.

Like a fiend in a cloud
  With howling woe,
After night I do crowd
  And with night will go;
I turn my back to the east
From whence comforts have increased;
For light doth seize my brain
With frantic pain.
SONG.

FRESH from the dewy hill, the merry year
Smiles on my head and mounts his flaming car;
Round my young brows the laurel wreathes a shade
And rising glories beam around my head.

My feet are wing'd while o'er the dewy lawn
I meet my maiden risen like the morn.
Oh bless those holy feet, like angels' feet;
Oh bless those limbs, beaming with heavenly light!

Like as an angel glittering in the sky
In times of innocence and holy joy;
The joyful shepherd stops his grateful song
To hear the music of an angel's tongue.

So when she speaks, the voice of Heaven I hear;
So when we walk, nothing impure comes near;
Each field seems Eden, and each calm retreat;
Each village seems the haunt of holy feet.
But that sweet village, where my black-eyed maid
Closes her eyes in sleep beneath night's shade,
Whene'er I enter, more than mortal fire

13

Burns in my soul, and does my song inspire.

SONG.

WHEN early morn walks forth in sober gray,
Then to my black-eyed maid I haste away,
When evening sits beneath her dusky bower
And gently sighs away the silent hour,
The village bell alarms, away I go,
And the vale darkens at my pensive woe.

To that sweet village, where my black-eyed maid
Doth drop a tear beneath the silent shade,
I turn my eyes; and pensive as I go
Curse my black stars, and bless my pleasing woe.

Oft when the summer sleeps among the trees,
Whispering faint murmurs to the scanty breeze,
I walk the village round; if at her side
A youth doth walk in stolen joy and pride,
I curse my stars in bitter grief and woe,
That made my love so high, and me so low.

O should she e'er prove false, his limbs I'd tear,
And throw all pity on the burning air;
I'd curse bright fortune for my mixed lot,
And then I'd die in peace, and be forgot.

TO THE MUSES.

WHETHER on Ida's shady brow
　　Or in the chambers of the East,
The chambers of the Sun, that now
　　From ancient melody have ceased;

Whether in heaven ye wander fair
　　Or the green corners of the earth,
Or the blue regions of the air,
　　Where the melodious winds have birth;

Whether on crystal rocks ye rove,
　　Beneath the bosom of the sea
Wandering in many a coral grove,
　　Fair Nine, forsaking Poetry;

How have you left the ancient love
　　That bards of old enjoy'd in you!
The languid strings do scarcely move,
　　The sound is forced, the notes are few!

GWIN, KING OF NORWAY.

COME, Kings, and listen to my song:
　When Gwin, the son of Nore,
Over the nations of the North
　His cruel sceptre bore;

The Nobles of the land did feed
　Upon the hungry poor;
They tear the poor man's lamb, and drive
　The needy from their door!

The land is desolate; our wives
　And children cry for bread;
Arise, and pull the tyrant down,
　Let Gwin be humbled.

Gordred the giant roused himself
　From sleeping in his cave;
He shook the hills, and in the clouds
　The troubled banners wave.
Beneath them roll'd, like tempests black,
　The numerous sons of blood;
Like lions' whelps, roaring abroad,
　Seeking their nightly food.

Down Bleron's hills they dreadful rush,
　Their cry ascends the clouds;
The trampling horse and clanging arms
　Like rushing mighty floods!

Their wives and children, weeping loud,
　Follow in wild array,
Howling like ghosts, furious as wolves
　In the bleak wintry day.

"Pull down the tyrant to the dust,
　"Let Gwin be humbled,"
They cry, " and let ten thousand lives
　"Pay for the tyrant's head."

From tower to tower the watchmen cry,
　"O Gwin, the son of Nore,
"Arouse thyself! the nations black
　"Like clouds, come rolling o'er!"
Gwin rear'd his shield, his palace shakes,
　His chiefs come rushing round;
Each, like an awful thunder-cloud
　With voice of solemn sound:

Like reared stones around a grave
　They stand around the King;
Then suddenly each seized his spear,
　And clashing steel does ring.

17

The husbandman does leave his plough
 To wade thro' fields of gore;
The merchant binds his brows in steel,
 And leaves the trading shore;

The shepherd leaves his mellow pipe,
 And sounds the trumpet shrill,
The workman throws his hammer down
 To heave the bloody bill.

Like the tall ghost of Barraton
 Who sports in stormy sky,
Gwin leads his host as black as night,
 When pestilence does fly,
With horses and with chariots—
 And all his spearmen bold,
March to the sound of mournful song,
 Like clouds around him roll'd.

Gwin lifts his hand—the nations halt;
 "Prepare for war," he cries—
Gordred appears!—his frowning brow
 Troubles our northern skies.

The armies stand, like balances
 Held in the Almighty's hand;—
"Gwin, thou hast fill'd thy measure up,
 "Thou'rt swept from out the land."

And now the raging armies rush'd
 Like warring mighty seas;
The Heavens are shook with roaring war,
 The dust ascends the skies!

Earth smokes with blood, and groans, and shakes,
 To drink her children's gore,
A sea of blood; nor can the eye
 See to the trembling shore.
And on the verge of this wild sea
 Famine and death doth cry;
The cries of women and of babes
 Over the field doth fly.

The king is seen raging afar,
 With all his men of might;
Like blazing comets scattering death
 Thro' the red feverous night.

Beneath his arm like sheep they die,
 And groan upon the plain;
The battle faints, and bloody men
 Fight upon hills of slain.

Now death is sick, and riven men.
 Labour and toil for life;

Steed rolls on steed, and shield on shield,
  Sunk in this sea of strife!

The god of war is drunk with blood,
  The earth doth faint and fail;
The stench of blood makes sick the heavens,
  Ghosts glut the throat of hell!
O what have Kings to answer for
  Before that awful throne!
When thousand deaths for vengeance cry
  And ghosts accusing groan!

Like blazing comets in the sky
  That shake the stars of light,
Which drop like fruit unto the earth
  Thro' the fierce burning night;

Like these did Gwin and Gordred meet,
  And the first blow decides;
Down from the brow unto the breast
  Gordred his head divides!

Gwin fell: the Sons of Norway fled,
  All that remain'd alive;
The rest did fill the vale of death,
  For them the eagles strive.

The river Dorman roll'd their blood
  Into the northern sea;
Who mourn'd his sons, and overwhelm'd
  The pleasant south country.

AN IMITATION OF SPENSER.

GOLDEN Apollo, that thro' heaven wide
Scatter'st the rays of light, and truth his beams,
In lucent words my darkling verses dight
And wash my earthy mind in thy clear streams,
That wisdom may descend in fairy dreams:
All while the jocund hours in thy train
Scatter their fancies at thy poet's feet;
And when thou yield'st to night thy wide domain,
Let rays of truth enlight his sleeping brain.

For brutish Pan in vain might thee assay
With tinkling sounds to dash thy nervous verse,
Sound without sense; yet in his rude affray,
(For Ignorance is Folly's leasing nurse,
And love of Folly needs none other's curse;)
Midas the praise hath gain'd of lengthen'd ears,
For which himself might deem him ne'er the worse
To sit in council with his modern peers
And judge of tinkling rhymes and elegances terse.

And thou, Mercurius, that with winged bow
Dost mount aloft into the yielding sky,
And thro' Heaven's halls thy airy flight dost throw,
Entering with holy feet to where on high
Jove weighs the counsel of futurity;
Then, laden with eternal fate, dost go
Down, like a falling star, from autumn sky,
And o'er the surface of the silent deep dost fly:

If thou arrivest at the sandy shore
Where nought but envious hissing adders dwell,
Thy golden rod, thrown on the dusty floor,
Can charm to harmony with potent spell;
Such is sweet Eloquence, that does dispel
Envy and Hate, that thirst for human gore;
And cause in sweet society to dwell
Vile savage minds that lurk in lonely cell.

O Mercury, assist my labouring sense
That round the circle of the world would fly,
As the wing'd eagle scorns the towery fence
Of Alpine hills round his high aëry,
And searches thro' the corners of the sky,
Sports in the clouds to hear the thunder's sound
And see the winged lightnings as they fly;
Then, bosom'd in an amber cloud, around
Plumes his wide wings, and seeks Sol's palace high.

And thou, O warrior Maid invincible,

Arm'd with the terrors of Almighty Jove.
Pallas, Minerva, maiden terrible,
Lovest thou to walk the peaceful solemn grove,
In solemn gloom of branches interwove?
Or bear'st thy Ægis o'er the burning field,
Where, like the sea, the waves of battle move?
Or have thy soft piteous eyes beheld
The weary wanderer thro' the desert rove?
Or does th' afflicted man thy heavenly bosom move?

BLIND-MAN'S BUFF.

WHEN silver snow decks Susan's clothes,
And jewel hangs at th' shepherd's nose,
The blushing bank is all my care,
With hearth so red, and walls so fair.
"Heap the sea-coal, come, heap it higher,
"The oaken log lay on the fire:"
The well-wash'd stools, a circling row,
With lad and lass, how fair the show!
The merry can of nut-brown ale,
The laughing jest, the love-sick tale,
Till, tired of chat, the game begins,
The lasses prick the lads with pins;
Roger from Dolly twitch'd the stool,
She falling, kiss'd the ground, poor fool!
She blush'd so red, with side-long glance
At hobnail Dick, who grieved the chance.
But now for Blind-man's Buff they call;
Of each incumbrance clear the hall—
Jenny her silken kerchief folds,
And blear-eyed Will the black lot holds,
Now laughing, stops, with "Silence, hush!"
And Peggy Pout gives Sam a push.—
The Blind-man's arms, extended wide,
Sam slips between:—"O woe betide
Thee, clumsy Will!—"but tittering Kate
Is penn'd up in the corner strait!
And now Will's eyes beheld the play,
He thought his face was t'other way.
"Now, Kitty, now; what chance hast thou,
"Roger so near thee trips, I vow!"
She catches him—then Roger ties
His own head up—but not his eyes;
For thro' the slender cloth he sees,
And runs at Sam, who slips with ease
His clumsy hold; and, dodging round,
Sukey is tumbled on the ground!—
"See what it is to play unfair!
"Where cheating is, there's mischief there"
But Roger still pursues the chace,—
"He sees! he sees!" cries softly Grace;
"O Roger, thou, unskill'd in art
"Must, surer bound, go thro' thy part!"
Now Kitty, pert, repeats the rhymes
And Roger turns him round three times,
Then pauses ere he starts; but Dick
Was mischief-bent upon a trick;
Down on his hands and knees he lay
Directly in the Blind-man's way,
Then cries out, "Hem!" Hodge heard, and ran
With hood-wink'd chance—sure of his man;
But down he came.—Alas, how frail
Our best of hopes, how soon they fail!

With crimson drops he stains the ground,
Confusion startles all around!
Poor piteous Dick supports his head,
And fain would cure the hurt he made;
But Kitty hasted with a key
And down his back they straight convey
The cold relief—the blood is stay'd
And Hodge again holds up his head.
Such are the fortunes of the game,
And those who play should stop the same
By wholesome laws, such as—all those
Who on the blinded man impose,
Stand in his stead; as long agone
When men were first a nation grown,
Lawless they lived, till wantonness
And liberty began t' increase,
And one man lay in another's way;
Then laws were made to keep fair play.

KING EDWARD THE THIRD.

Poetical sketches reprint 59 (detail 2).png

PERSONS.

King Edward.

The Black Prince.

Queen Philippa.

Duke of Clarence.

Sir John Chandos.

Sir Thomas Dagworth.

Sir Walter Manny.

Lord Audley.

Lord Percy.

Bishop.

William, Dagworth's man.

Peter Blunt, a common soldier.

Poetical sketches reprint 61 (detail).png

KING EDWARD THE THIRD.

SCENE. The Coast of France, King Edward and Nobles before it. The Army.

King.

O THOU to whose fury the nations are
But as dust! maintain thy servant's right.
Without thine aid, the twisted mail, and spear,
And forged helm, and shield of seven times beaten brass,
Are idle trophies of the vanquisher.
When confusion rages, when the field is in a flame,
When the cries of blood tear horror from heaven,
And yelling death runs up and down the ranks,

Let Liberty, the charter'd right of Englishmen,
Won by our fathers in many a glorious field,
Enerve my soldiers; let Liberty
Blaze in each countenance, and fire the battle.
The enemy fight in chains, invisible chains, but heavy;
Their minds are fetter'd; then how can they be free,
While, like the mounting flame,
We spring to battle o'er the floods of death?
And these fair youths, the flower of England,
Venturing their lives in my most righteous cause,
O sheathe their hearts with triple steel, that they
May emulate their fathers' virtues.
And thou, my son, be strong; thou fightest for a crown
That death can never ravish from thy brow,
A crown of glory but from thy very dust
Shall beam a radiance, to fire the breasts
Of youth unborn! Our names are written equal
In fame's wide-trophied hall; 'tis ours to gild
The letters, and to make them shine with gold
That never tarnishes: whether Third Edward,
Or the Prince of Wales, or Montacute, or Mortimer,
Or ev'n the least by birth, shall gain the brightest fame,
Is in His hand to whom all men are equal
The world of men are like the numerous stars
That beam and twinkle in the depth of night,
Each clad in glory according to his sphere;
But we, that wander from our native seats
And beam forth lustre on a darkling world,
Grow large as we advance! and some perhaps
The most obscure at home, that scarce were seen
To twinkle in their sphere, may so advance,
That the astonish'd world, with upturn'd eyes,
Regardless of the moon, and those that once were bright,
Stand only for to gaze upon their splendour!
[He here knights the Prince and other
young Nobles.

Now let us take a just revenge for those
Brave Lords, who fell beneath the bloody axe
At Paris. Thanks, noble Harcourt, for 'twas
By your advice we landed here in Brittany,
A country not yet sown with destruction,
And where the fiery whirlwind of swift war
Has not yet swept its desolating wing.—
Into three parties we divide by day
And separate march, but join again at night:
Each knows his rank, and Heaven marshal all.
[Exeunt.

SCENE. English Court; Lionel, Duke of Clarence, Queen Philippa, Lords, Bishop, &c.

Clarence.

MY Lords, I have by the advice of her

25

Whom I am doubly bound to obey, my Parent
And my Sovereign, called you together.
My task is great, my burden heavier than
My unfledged years;
Yet with your kind assistance, Lords, I hope
England shall dwell in peace: that while my father
Toils in his wars and turns his eyes on this
His native shore, and sees commerce fly round
With his white wings,[1] and sees his golden London
And her silver Thames, throng'd with shining spires
And corded ships, her merchants buzzing round
Like summer bees, and all the golden cities
In his land, overflowing with honey,
Glory may not be dimm'd with clouds of care.
Say, Lords, should not our thoughts be first to commerce?
My Lord Bishop, you would recommend us agriculture?

Bishop.

Sweet Prince, the arts of peace are great,
And no less glorious than those of war,
Perhaps more glorious in the philosophic mind.
When I sit at my home, a private man,
My thoughts are on my gardens and my fields,
How to employ the hand that lacketh bread.
If Industry is in my diocese
Religion will flourish; each man's heart
Is cultivated and will bring forth fruit:
This is my private duty and my pleasure.
But as I sit in council with my prince,
My thoughts take in the general good of the whole,
And England is the land favour'd by Commerce;
For Commerce, tho' the child of Agriculture,
Fosters his parent, who else must sweat and toil
And gain but scanty fare. Then, my dear Lord,
Be England's trade our care; and we, as tradesmen,
Looking to the gain of this our native land.

Clarence.

O my good Lord, true wisdom drops like honey
From your tongue, as from a worshipp'd oak!
Forgive, my Lords, my talkative youth, that speaks
Not merely what my narrow observation has
Pick'd up, but what I have concluded from your lessons:
Now, by the Queen's advice, I ask your leave
To dine to-morrow with the Mayor of London:
If I obtain your leave, I have another boon
To ask, which is the favour of your company.
I fear Lord Percy will not give me leave.

Percy.

Dear Sir, a prince should always keep his state,
And grant his favours with a sparing hand,
Or they are never rightly valued.
These are my thoughts: yet it were best to go:
But keep a proper dignity, for now
You represent the sacred person of
Your father; 'tis with princes as 'tis with the sun;
If not sometimes o'erclouded, we grow weary
Of his officious glory.

Clarence.

Then you will give me leave to shine sometimes,
My Lord?
Lord.

Thou hast a gallant spirit, which I fear
Will be imposed on by the closer sort![Aside.

Clarence.

Well, I'll endeavour to take
Lord Percy's advice; I have been used so much
To dignity, that I'm sick on't.

Queen Philippa.

Fie, fie, Lord Clarence, you proceed not to business,
But speak of your own pleasures.
I hope their lordships will excuse your giddiness.

Clarence.

My Lords, the French have fitted out many
Small ships of war that, like to ravening wolves,
Infest our English seas, devouring all
Our burden'd vessels, spoiling our naval flocks.
The merchants do complain, and beg our aid.

Percy.

The merchants are rich enough;
Can they not help themselves?

Bishop.

They can, and may; but how to gain their will
Requires our countenance and help.

Percy.

When that they find they must, my Lord, they will
Let them but suffer awhile, and you shall see
They will bestir themselves.

Bishop.

Lord Percy cannot mean that we should suffer
This disgrace: if so, we are not sovereigns
Of the sea: our right, that Heaven gave
To England, when at the birth of Nature
She was seated in the deep, the Ocean ceased
His mighty roar, and, fawning, play'd around
Her snowy feet, and own'd his awful Queen.
Lord Percy, if the heart is sick, the head
Must be aggrieved; if but one member suffer,
The heart doth fail. You say, my Lord, the merchants
Can, if they will, defend themselves against
These rovers: this is a noble scheme,
Worthy the brave Lord Percy, and as worthy
His generous aid to put it into practice.
Percy.

Lord Bishop, what was rash in me, is wise
In you; I dare not own the plan. 'Tis not
Mine. Yet will I, if you please,
Quickly to the Lord Mayor, and work him onward
To this most glorious voyage; on which cast
I'll set my whole estate,
But we will bring these Gallic rovers under.

Queen Philippa.

Thanks, brave Lord Percy; you have the thanks
Of England's Queen, and will, ere long, of England.
[Exeunt.

SCENE. At Cressy. Sir Thomas Dagworth and Lord Audley meeting.

Audley.

GOOD-MORROW, brave Sir Thomas; the bright morn
Smiles on our army, and the gallant sun
Springs from the hills like a young hero
Into the battle, shaking his golden locks
Exultingly: this is a promising day.
Dagworth.

28

Why, my Lord Audley, I don't know.
Give me your hand, and now I'll tell you what
I think you do not know. Edward's afraid of Philip.

Audley.

Ha! Ha! Sir Thomas! you but joke;
Did you e'er see him fear? At Blanchetaque,
When almost singly he drove six thousand
French from the ford, did he fear then?

Dagworth.

Yes, fear—that made him fight so.

Audley.

By the same reason I might say 'tis fear
That makes you fight.

Dagworth.

Mayhap you may: look upon Edward's face,
No one can say he fears; but when he turns
His back, then I will say it to his face;
He is afraid: he makes us all afraid.
I cannot bear the enemy at my back.
Now here we are at Cressy; where to-morrow,
To-morrow we shall know. I say, Lord Audley,
That Edward runs away from Philip.

Audley.

Perhaps you think the Prince too is afraid?

Dagworth.

No; God forbid! I'm sure he is not.
He is a young lion. O I have seen him fight
And give command, and lightning has flash'd
From his eyes across the field: I have seen him
Shake hands with death, and strike a bargain for
The enemy; he has danced in the field
Of battle, like the youth at morris-play.
I'm sure he's not afraid, nor Warwick, nor none,
None of us but me, and I am very much afraid.

Audley.

Are you afraid too, Sir Thomas?
I believe that as much as I believe.
The King's afraid: but what are you afraid of?

Dagworth.

Of having my back laid open; we turn
Our backs to the fire, till we shall burn our skirts.
Audley.

And this, Sir Thomas, you call fear? Your fear
Is of a different kind then from the King's;
He fears to turn his face, and you to turn your back.
I do not think, Sir Thomas, you know what fear is.

Enter Sir John Chandos.

Chandos.

Good-morrow, Generals; I give you joy:
Welcome to the fields of Cressy. Here we stop,
And wait for Philip.

Dagworth.

I hope so.

Audley.

There, Sir Thomas; do you call that fear?

Dagworth.

I don't know; perhaps he takes it by fits.
Why, noble Chandos, look you here—
One rotten sheep spoils the whole flock;
And if the bell-wether is tainted, I wish
The Prince may not catch the distemper too.
Chandos.

Distemper, Sir Thomas! what distemper?
I have not heard.

Dagworth.

Why, Chandos, you are a wise man,
I know you understand me; a distemper
The King caught here in France of running away.

Audley.

Sir Thomas, you say you have caught it too.

Dagworth.

And so will the whole army; 'tis very catching,
For when the coward runs, the brave man totters.
Perhaps the air of the country is the cause.
I feel it coming upon me, so I strive against it;
You yet are whole; but after a few more
Retreats, we all shall know how to retreat
Better than fight.—To be plain, I think retreating
Too often, takes away a soldier's courage.

Chandos.

Here comes the King himself: tell him your thoughts
Plainly, Sir Thomas.
Dagworth.

I've told him before, but his disorder
Makes him deaf.

Enter King Edward and Black Prince.

King.

Good-morrow, Generals; when English courage fails,
Down goes our right to France.
But we are conquerors everywhere; nothing
Can stand our soldiers; each man is worthy
Of a triumph. Such an army of heroes
Ne'er shouted to the Heavens, nor shook the field.
Edward, my son, thou art
Most happy, having such command: the man
Were base who were not fired to deeds
Above heroic, having such examples.

Prince.

Sire, with respect and deference I look
Upon such noble souls, and wish myself
Worthy the high command that heaven and you
Have given me. When I have seen the field glow,

And in each countenance the soul of war
Curb'd by the manliest reason, I have been wing'd
With certain victory; and 'tis my boast,
And shall be still my glory. I was inspired
By these brave troops.

Dagworth.

Your Grace had better make them
All Generals.

King.

Sir Thomas Dagworth, you must have your joke,
And shall, while you can fight as you did at
The Ford.

Dagworth.

I have a small petition to your Majesty.

King.

What can Sir Thomas Dagworth ask
That Edward can refuse?

Dagworth.

I hope your Majesty cannot refuse so great
A trifle; I've gilt your cause with my best blood,
And would again, were I not forbid
By him whom I am bound to obey: my hands
Are tied up, my courage shrunk and wither'd,
My sinews slacken'd, and my voice scarce heard;
Therefore I beg I may return to England.

King.

I know not what you could have ask'd, Sir Thomas,
That I would not have sooner parted with
Than such a soldier as you have been, and such a friend:
Nay, I will know the most remote particulars
Of this your strange petition; that, if I can,
I still may keep you here.

Dagworth.

Here on the fields of Cressy we are settled

32

Till Philip springs the timorous covey again.
The wolf is hunted down by causeless fear;
The lion flees, and fear usurps his heart
Startled, astonish'd at the clamorous cock;
The Eagle, that doth gaze upon the sun,
Fears the small fire that plays about the fen;
If, at this moment of their idle fear,
The dog doth seize the wolf, the forester the lion,
The negro in the crevice of the rock
Doth seize the soaring eagle; undone by flight,
They tame submit: such the effect flight has
On noble souls. Now hear its opposite:
The timorous stag starts from the thicket wild,
The fearful crane Springs from the splashy fen,
The shining snake glides o'er the bending grass,
The stag turns head, and bays the crying hounds;
The crane o'ertaken fighteth with the hawk;
The snake doth turn, and bite the padding foot.
And if your Majesty's afraid of Philip,
You are more like a lion than a crane:
Therefore I beg I may return to England.

King.

Sir Thomas, now I understand your mirth,
Which often plays with wisdom for its pastime,
And brings good counsel from the breast of laughter.
I hope you'll stay and see us fight this battle
And reap rich harvest in the fields of Cressy;
Then go to England, tell them how we fight,
And set all hearts on fire to be with us.
Philip is plumed, and thinks we flee from him,
Else he would never dare to attack us. Now,
Now the quarry's set! and Death doth sport
In the bright sunshine of this fatal day.

Dagworth.

Now my heart dances and I am as light
As the young bridegroom going to be married.
Now must I to my soldiers, get them ready,
Furbish our armours bright, new plume our helms;
And we will sing like the young housewives busied
In the dairy; my feet are wing'd, but not
For flight, an please your grace.

King.

If all my soldiers are as pleased as you,
'Twill be a gallant thing to fight or die;
Then I can never be afraid of Philip.

Dagworth.

A raw-boned fellow t' other day pass'd by me;
I told him to put off his hungry looks—
He answer'd me, "I hunger for another battle."
I saw a little Welshman with a fiery face;
I told him he look'd like a candle half
Burn'd out; he answer'd, he was "pig enough
"To light another pattle." Last night, beneath
The moon I walk'd abroad, when all had pitch'd
Their tents, and all were still;
I heard a blooming youth singing a song
He had composed, and at each pause he wiped
His dropping eyes. The ditty was, "if he
"Return'd victorious, he should wed a maiden
"Fairer than snow, and rich as midsummer."
Another wept, and wish'd health to his father.
I chid them both, but gave them noble hopes.
These are the minds that glory in the battle,
And leap and dance to hear the trumpet sound.

King.

Sir Thomas Dagworth, be thou near our person;
Thy heart is richer than the vales of France:
I will not part with such a man as thee.
If Philip came arm'd in the ribs of death,
And shook his mortal dart against my head,
Thou'dst laugh his fury into nerveless shame!
Go now, for thou art suited to the work,
Throughout the camp; inflame the timorous,
Blow up the sluggish into ardour, and
Confirm the strong with strength, the weak inspire,
And wing their brows with hope and expectation:
Then to our tent return, and meet to council.
[Exit Dagworth.

Chandos.

That man's a hero in his closet, and more
A hero to the servants of his house
Than to the gaping world; he carries windows
In that enlarged breast of his, that all
May see what's done within.
Prince.

He is a genuine Englishman, my Chandos,
And hath the spirit of Liberty within him.
Forgive my prejudice, Sir John; I think
My Englishmen the bravest people on
· face of the earth.

Chandos.

Courage, my Lord, proceeds from self-dependence;
Teach man to think he's a free agent,
Give but a slave his liberty, he'll shake
Off sloth, and build himself a hut, and hedge
A spot of ground; this he'll defend; 'tis his
By right of nature: thus set in action,
He will still move onward to plan conveniences,
Till glory fires his breast to enlarge his castle,
While the poor slave drudges all day, in hope
To rest at night.

King.

Liberty, how glorious art thou!
I see thee hovering o'er my army, with
Thy wide-stretch'd plumes; I see thee
Lead them on to battle;
I see thee blow thy golden trumpet while
Thy sons shout the strong shout of victory!
O noble Chandos, think thyself a gardener,
My son a vine, which I commit unto
Thy care; prune all extravagant shoots, and guide
The ambitious tendrils in the path of wisdom;
Water him with thy advice, and Heaven
Rain freshening dew upon his branches. And,
O Edward, my dear son! learn to think lowly of
Thyself, as we may all each prefer other—
'Tis the best policy, and 'tis our duty.
[Exit King Edward.

Prince.

And may our duty, Chandos, be our pleasure.—
Now we are alone, Sir John, I will unburden
And breathe my hopes into the burning air,
Where thousand deaths are posting up and down,
Commission'd to this fatal field of Cressy.
Methinks I see them arm my gallant soldiers,
And gird the sword upon each thigh, and fit
Each shining helm, and string each stubborn bow,
And dance to the neighing of our steeds.
Methinks the shout begins, the battle burns;
Methinks I see them perch on English crests,
And roar the wild flame of fierce war upon
The thronged enemy! In truth, I am too full;
It is my sin to love the noise of war.
Chandos, thou seest my weakness; strong nature
Will bend or break us: my blood, like a springtide,
Does rise so high to overflow all bounds
Of moderation; while Reason, in her frail bark,
Can see no shore or bound for vast ambition.

35

Come, take the helm, my Chandos,
That my full-blown sails overset me not
In the wild tempest. Condemn my venturous youth
That plays with danger, as the innocent child,
Unthinking, plays upon the viper's den:
I am a coward in my reason, Chandos.

Chandos.

You are a man, my prince, and a brave man,
If I can judge of actions; but your heat
Is the effect of youth, and want of use:
Use makes the armed field and noisy war
Pass over as a summer cloud, unregarded,
Or but expected as a thing of course.
Age is contemplative; each rolling year
Brings forth fruit to the mind's treasure-house;
While vacant youth doth crave and seek about
Within itself, and findeth discontent,
Then, tired of thought, impatient takes the wing,
Seizes the fruits of time, attacks experience,
Roams round vast Nature's forest, where no bounds
Are set, the swiftest may have room, the strongest
Find prey; till tired at length, sated and tired
With the changing sameness, old variety,
We sit us down, and view our former joys
With distaste and dislike.

Prince.

Then if we must tug for experience
Let us not fear to beat round Nature's wilds
And rouse the strongest prey: then if we fall,
We fall with glory. I know the wolf
Is dangerous to fight, not good for food,
Nor is the hide a comely vestment; so
We have our battle for our pains. I know
That youth has need of age to point fit prey,
And oft the stander-by shall steal the fruit
Of the other's labour. This is philosophy;
These are the tricks of the world; but the pure soul
Shall mount on native wings, disdaining little sport,
And cut a path into the heaven of glory,
Leaving a track of light for men to wonder at.
I'm glad my father does not hear me talk;
You can find friendly excuses for me, Chandos;
But do you not think, Sir John, that if it please
The Almighty to stretch out my span of life,
I shall with pleasure view a glorious action,
Which my youth master'd?

Chandos.

Considerate age, my Lord, views motives,
And not acts; when neither warbling voice
Nor trilling pipe is heard, nor pleasure sits
With trembling age, the voice of Conscience then,
Sweeter than music in a summer's eve,
Shall warble round the snowy head, and keep
Sweet symphony to feather'd angels, sitting
As guardians round your chair; then shall the pulse
Beat slow, and taste, and touch, and sight, and sound, and smell,
That sing and dance round Reason's fine-wrought throne,
Shall flee away, and leave him all forlorn;
Yet not forlorn if Conscience is his friend.
[Exeunt.

SCENE. In Sir Thomas Dagworth's Tent. Dagworth and William his man.

Dagworth.

BRING hither my armour, William;
Ambition is the growth of every clime.

William.

Does it grow in England, sir?

Dagworth.

Ay, it grows most in lands most cultivated.

William.

Then it grows most in France; the vines here
Are finer than any we have in England.

Dagworth.

Ay, but the oaks are not.

William.

What is the tree you mentioned? I don't think
I ever saw it.

Dagworth.

Ambition.

William.

Is it a little creeping root that grows in ditches?

Dagworth.

Thou dost not understand me, William.
It is a root that grows in every breast;
Ambition is the desire or passion that one man
Has to get before another, in any pursuit after glory;
But I don't think you have any of it.

William.

Yes, I have; I have a great ambition to know everything, sir.

Dagworth.

But when our first ideas are wrong, what follows must all be wrong, of course; 'tis best to know a little, and to know that little aright.

William.

Then, sir, I should be glad to know if it was not ambition that brought over our king to France to fight for his right?

Dagworth.

Though the knowledge of that will not profit thee much, yet I will tell you that it was ambition.

William.

Then if ambition is a sin, we are all guilty in coming with him, and in fighting for him.

Dagworth.

Now, William, thou dost thrust the question home; but I must tell you that guilt being an act of the mind, none are guilty but those whose minds are prompted by that same ambition.

William.

Now, I always thought that a man might be guilty of doing wrong without knowing it was wrong.

Dagworth.

Thou art a natural philosopher, and knowest truth by instinct; while reason runs aground, as we have run our argument. Only remember, William, all have it in their power to know the motives of their own actions, and 'tis a sin to act without some reason.

William.

And whoever acts without reason may do a great deal of harm without knowing it.

Dagworth.

Thou art an endless moralist.

William.

Now there's a story come into my head, that I will tell your honour, if you'll give me leave.

Dagworth.

No, William, save it till another time; this is no time for story-telling; but here comes one who is as entertaining as a good story.

Enter Peter Blunt.

Peter.

Yonder's a musician going to play before the King; it's a new song about the French and English, and the Prince has made the minstrel a squire, and given him I don't know what, and I can't tell whether he don't mention us all one by one; and he is to write another about all us that are to die, that we may be remembered in Old England, for all our blood and bones are in France; and a great deal more that we shall all hear by and by; and I came to tell your honour, because you love to hear war-songs.

Dagworth.

And who is this minstrel, Peter, dost know?

Peter.

O ay, I forgot to tell that; he has got the same name as Sir John Chandos that the prince is always with—the wise man that knows us all as well as your honour, only ain't so good-natured.

Dagworth.

I thank you, Peter, for your imformation, but not for your compliment, which is not true: there's as much difference between him and me as between glittering sand and fruitful mould; or shining glass and a wrought diamond, set in rich gold, and fitted to the finger of an Emperor; such is that worthy Chandos.

Peter.

I know your honour does not think anything of yourself, but everybody else does.

Dagworth.

Go, Peter, get you gone; flattery is delicious, even from the lips of a babbler.

|Exit Peter.

William.

I never flatter your honour.

Dagworth.

I don't know that.

William.

Why you know, sir, when we were in England, at the tournament at Windsor, and the Earl of Warwick was tumbled over, you asked me if he did not look well when he fell? and I said no, he looked very foolish; and you were very angry with me for not flattering you.

Dagworth.

You mean that I was angry with you for not flattering the Earl of Warwick.|Exeunt.

40

SCENE. Sir Thomas Dagworth's Tent; Sir Thomas Dagworth. To him enters Sir Walter Manny.

Sir Walter.

SIR THOMAS DAGWORTH, I have been weeping
Over the men that are to die to-day.

Dagworth.

Why, brave Sir Walter, you or I may fall.

Sir Walter.

I know this breathing flesh must lie and rot,
Cover'd with silence and forgetfulness;
Death roams in cities' smoke, and in still night,
When men sleep in their beds, walketh about!
How many in walled cities lie and groan,
Turning themselves upon their beds,
Talking with death, answering his hard demands!
How many walk in darkness, terrors are round
The curtains of their beds, destruction is
Ready at the door! How many sleep
In earth, cover'd with stones and deathy dust,
Resting in quietness, whose spirits walk
Upon the clouds of heaven, to die no more.
Yet death is terrible, tho' borne on angels' wings.
How terrible then is the field of death,
Where he doth rend the vault of heaven,
And shake the gates of hell!
O Dagworth, France is sick; the very sky,
Tho' sunshine light it, seems to me as pale
As the pale fainting man on his death-bed,
Whose face is shewn by light of sickly taper.
It makes me sad and sick at very heart;
Thousands must fall to-day.

Dagworth.

Thousands of souls must leave this prison-house,
To be exalted to those heavenly fields,
Where songs of triumph, palms of victory,
Where peace, and joy, and love, and calm content,
Sit singing in the azure clouds, and strew
Flowers of heaven's growth over the banquet-table,
Bind ardent hope upon your feet like shoes,
Put on the robe of preparation,
The table is prepared in shining heaven,

The flowers of immortality are blown;
Let those that fight fight in good stedfastness,
And those that fall shall rise in victory.

Sir Walter.

I've often seen the burning field of war,
And often heard the dismal clang of arms;
But never, till this fatal day of Cressy,
Has my soul fainted with these views of death.
I seem to be in one great charnel-house,
And seem to scent the rotten carcases:
I seem to hear the dismal yells of death,
While the black gore drops from his horrid jaws:
Yet I not fear the monster in his pride—
But oh! the souls that are to die to-day!

Dagworth.

Stop, brave Sir Walter; let me drop a tear,
Then let the clarion of war begin;
I'll fight and weep, 'tis in my country's cause;
I'll weep and shout for glorious liberty.
Grim war shall laugh and shout, decked in tears,
And blood shall flow like streams across the meadows,
That murmur down their pebbly channels, and
Spend their sweet lives to do their country service:
Then shall England's verdure shoot, her fields shall smile,
Her ships shall sing across the foaming sea,
Her mariners shall use the flute and viol,
And rattling guns, and black and dreary war,
Shall be no more.

Sir Walter.

Well, let the trumpet sound, and the drum beat;
Let war stain the blue heavens with bloody banners;
I'll draw my sword, nor ever sheathe it up
Till England blow the trump of victory,
Or I lie stretch'd upon the field of death.[Exeunt.

SCENE. In the Camp. Several of the Warriors met at the King's Tent with a Minstrel, who sings the following Song:

O SONS of Trojan Brutus, clothed in war,
Whose voices are the thunder of the field,
Rolling dark clouds o'er France, muffling the sun
In sickly darkness like a dim eclipse,
Threatening as the red brow of storms, as fire
Burning up nations in your wrath and fury:

Your ancestors came from the fires of Troy
(Like lions roused by lightning from their dens,
Whose eyes do glare against the stormy fires),
Heated with war, fill'd with the blood of Greeks,
With helmets hewn, and shields covered with gore,
In navies black, broken with wind and tide:

They landed in firm array upon the rocks
Of Albion; they kiss'd the rocky shore;
"Be thou our mother and our nurse," they said;
"Our children's mother, and thou shalt be our grave,
"The sepulchre of ancient Troy, from whence
"Shall rise cities, and thrones, and arms, and awful powers."
Our fathers swarm from the ships. Giant voices
Are heard from the hills, the enormous sons
Of Ocean run from rocks and caves; wild men,
Naked and roaring like lions, hurling rocks,
And wielding knotty clubs, like oaks entangled
Thick as a forest, ready for the axe.

Our fathers move in firm array to battle,
The savage monsters rush like roaring fire;
Like as a forest roars with crackling flames
When the red lightning, borne by furious storms,
Lights on some woody shore; the parched heavens
Rain fire into the molten raging sea:

The smoking trees are strewn upon the shore,
Spoil'd of their verdure! O how oft have they
Defied the storm that howled o'er their heads.
Our fathers, sweating, lean on their spears, and view
The mighty dead: giant bodies, streaming blood,
Dread visages, frowning in silent death.

Then Brutus spoke, inspired; our fathers sit
Attentive on the melancholy shore:
Hear ye the voice of Brutus—"The flowing waves
"Of time come rolling o'er my breast," said;
"And my heart labours with futurity:
"Our sons shall rule the empire of the sea.
"Their mighty wings shall stretch from east to west,
"Their nest is in the sea; but they shall roam
"Like eagles for the prey; nor shall the young
"Crave or be heard; for plenty shall bring forth,
"Cities shall sing, and vales in rich array
"Shall laugh, whose fruitful laps bend down with fulness.

"Our sons shall rise from thrones in joy,
"Each one buckling on his armour; Morning
"Shall be prevented by their swords gleaming,
"And Evening hear their song of victory:
"Their towers shall be built upon the rocks,
"Their daughters shall sing, surrounded with shining spears.

"Liberty shall stand upon the cliffs of Albion,

43

"Casting her blue eyes over the green ocean;
"Or, towering, stand upon the roaring waves,
"Stretching her mighty spear o'er distant lands;
"While, with her eagle wings, she covereth
"Fair Albion's shore, and all her families."

1. Compare Tennyson: Exhibition Ode, 1862:
"Let the fair white-wing'd peacemaker fly
To happy havens under all the sky."

PROLOGUE

INTENDED FOE A DRAMATIC PIECE OF KING EDWARD
THE FOURTH.

O FOR a voice like thunder, and a tongue
To drown the throat of war! When the senses
Are shaken, and the soul is driven to madness,
Who can stand? When the souls of the oppressed
Fight in the troubled air that rages, who can stand?
When the whirlwind of fury comes from the
Throne of God, when the frowns of His countenance
Drive the nations together, who can stand?
When Sin claps his broad wings over the battle,
And sails rejoicing in the flood of death;
When souls are torn to everlasting fire,
And fiends of hell rejoice upon the slain,
O who can stand? O who hath caused this?
O who can answer at the throne of God?
The Kings and Nobles of the land have done it!
Hear it not, Heaven, thy ministers have done it!

JUSTICE hath heaved a sword to plunge in Albion's breast; for Albion's sins are crimson-dyed, and the red scourge follows her desolate sons. Then Patriot rose; full oft did Patriot rise, when Tyranny hath stained fair Albion's breast with her own children's gore. Round his majestic feet deep thunders roll: each heart does tremble, and each knee grows slack. The stars of heaven tremble; the roaring voice of war, the trumpet, calls to battle. Brother in brother's blood must bathe, rivers of death. O land most hapless! O beauteous island, how forsaken! Weep from thy silver fountains, weep from thy gentle rivers! The angel of the island weeps! Thy widowed virgins weep beneath thy shades! Thy aged fathers gird themselves for war! The sucking infant lives to die in battle; the weeping mother feeds him for the slaughter! The husbandman doth leave his bending harvest! Blood cries afar! The land doth sow itself! The glittering youth of courts must gleam in arms! The aged senators their ancient swords assume! The trembling sinews of old age must work the work of death against their progeny; for Tyranny hath stretched his purple arm, and "Blood," he cries: "The chariots and the horses, the noise of shout, and dreadful thunder of the battle heard afar!" Beware, O proud! thou shalt be humbled; thy cruel brow, thine iron heart is smitten, though lingering Fate is slow. O yet may Albion smile again, and stretch her peaceful arms, and raise her golden head, exultingly! Her citizens shall throng about her gates, her mariners shall sing upon the sea, and myriads shall to her temples crowd! Her sons shall joy as in the morning! Her daughters sing as to the rising year!

A WAR SONG

TO ENGLISHMEN.

PREPARE, prepare the iron helm of war,
Bring forth the lots, cast in the spacious orb;
The Angel of Fate turns them with mighty hands,
And casts them out upon the darken'd earth!
            Prepare, prepare.

Prepare your hearts for Death's cold hand! prepare
Your souls for flight, your bodies for the earth!
Prepare your arms for glorious victory!
Prepare your eyes to meet a holy God!
            Prepare, prepare.

Whose fatal scroll is that? Methinks 'tis mine!
Why sinks my heart, why faltereth my tongue?
Had I three lives, I 'd die in such a cause,
And rise, with ghosts, over the well-fought field.
            Prepare, prepare.

The arrows of Almighty God are drawn!
Angels of Death stand in the lowering heavens!
Thousands of souls must seek the realms of light,
And walk together on the clouds of heaven!
            Prepare, prepare.

Soldiers, prepare! Our cause is Heaven's cause;
Soldiers, prepare! Be worthy of our cause:
Prepare to meet our fathers in the sky:
Prepare, O troops that are to fall to-day!
            Prepare, prepare.

Alfred shall smile, and make his harp rejoice;
The Norman William and the learned Clerk,
And Lion-Heart, and black-brow'd Edward with
His loyal queen shall rise, and welcome us!
            Prepare, prepare.

THE veiled Evening walked solitary down the western hills, and Silence reposed in the valley; the birds of day were heard in their nests, rustling in brakes and thickets; and the owl and bat flew round the darkening trees: all is silent when Nature takes her repose.—In former times, on such an evening, when the cold clay breathed with life, and our ancestors, who now sleep in their graves, walked on the steadfast globe, the remains of a family of the tribes of Earth, a mother and a sister were gathered to the sick bed of a youth. Sorrow linked them together; leaning on one another's necks alternately—like lilies, dropping tears in each other's bosom, they stood by the bed like reeds bending over a lake, when the evening drops trickle down. His voice was low as the whisperings of the woods when the wind is asleep, and the visions of Heaven unfold their visitation. "Parting is hard, and death is terrible; I seem to walk through a deep valley, far from the light of day, alone and comfortless! The damps of death fall thick upon me! Horrors stare me in the face! I look behind, there is no returning; Death follows after me; I walk in regions of Death, where no tree is; without a lantern to direct my steps, without a staff to support me."—Thus he laments through the still evening, till the curtains of darkness were drawn! Like the sound of a broken pipe, the aged woman raised her voice. "O my son, my son, I know but little of the path thou goest! But lo, there is a God, who made the world; stretch out thy hand to Him." The youth replied, like a voice heard from a sepulchre, "My hand is feeble, how should I stretch it out? My ways are sinful, how should I raise mine eyes? My voice hath used deceit, how should I call on Him who is Truth? My breath is loathsome, how should He not be offended? If I lay my face in the dust, the grave opens its mouth for me; if I lift up my head, sin covers me as a cloak! O my dear friends, pray ye for me! stretch forth your hands, that my Helper may come! Through the void space I walk between the sinful world and eternity! Beneath me burns eternal fire! O for a hand to pluck me forth!" As the voice of an omen heard in the silent valley, when the few inhabitants cling trembling together; as the voice of the Angel of Death, when the thin beams of the moon give a faint light, such was this young man's voice to his friends. Like the bubbling waters of the brook in the dead of night, the aged woman raised her cry, and said, "O voice, that dwellest in my breast, can I not cry, and lift my eyes to heaven? Thinking of this, my spirit is turned within me into confusion. O my child, my child! is thy breath infected? so is mine. As the deer wounded, by the brooks of water, so the arrows of sin stick in my flesh; the poison hath entered into my marrow."—Like rolling waves upon a desert shore, sighs succeeded sighs; they covered their faces, and wept. The youth lay silent—his mother's arm was under his head; he was like a cloud tossed by the winds, till the sun shine, and the drops of rain glisten, the yellow harvest breathes, and the thankful eyes of the villagers are turned up in smiles—the traveller that hath taken shelter under an oak, eyes the distant country with joy. Such smiles were seen upon the face of the youth! a visionary hand wiped away his tears, and a ray of light beamed around his head! All was still. The moon hung not out her lamp, and the stars faintly glimmered in the summer sky; the breath of night slept among the leaves of the forest; the bosom of the lofty hill drank in the silent dew, while on his majestic brow the voice of angels is heard, and stringed sounds ride upon the wings of night. The sorrowful pair lift up their heads, hovering angels are around them, voices of comfort are heard over the Couch of Death, and the youth breathes out his soul with joy into eternity.

WHO is this, that with unerring step dares tempt the wilds, where only Nature's foot hath trod? 'Tis Contemplation, daughter of the grey Morning! Majestical she steppeth, and with her pure quill on every flower writeth Wisdom's name, now lowly bending, whispers in mine ear, "O man, how great, how little thou! O man, slave of each moment, lord of eternity! seest thou where Mirth sits on the painted cheek? doth it not seem ashamed of such a place, and grow immoderate to brave it out? O what an humble garb true Joy puts on! Those who want Happiness must stoop to find it; it is a flower that grows in every vale. Vain foolish man, that roams on lofty rocks, where, 'cause his garments are swoln with wind, he fancies he is grown into a giant! Lo, then, Humility, take it, and wear it in thine heart; lord of thyself, thou then art lord of all. Clamour brawls along the streets, and destruction hovers in the city's smoke; but on these plains, and in these silent woods, true joys descend: here build thy nest; here fix thy staff; delights blossom around; numberless beauties blow; the green grass springs in joy, and the nimble air kisses the leaves; the brook stretches its arms along the velvet meadow, its silver inhabitants sport and play. The youthful sun joys like a hunter roused to the chase: he rushes up the sky, and lays hold on the immortal coursers of day; the sky glitters with the jingling trappings! Like a triumph, season follows season, while the airy music fills the world with joyful sounds." I answered, "Heavenly goddess! I am wrapped in mortality, my flesh is a prison, my bones the bars of death, Misery builds over our cottage roofs, and Discontent runs like a brook. Even in childhood, sorrow slept with me in my cradle; he followed me up and down in the house when I grew up; he was my school-fellow: thus he was in my steps and in my play, till he became to me as my brother. I walked through dreary places with him, and in church-yards; and oft I found myself sitting by Sorrow on a tomb-stone."

SAMSON.

SAMSON, the strongest of the children of men, I sing; how he was foiled by woman's arts, by a false wife brought to the gates of death! O Truth, that shinest with propitious beams, turning our earthly night to heavenly day, from presence of the Almighty Father! thou visitest our darkling world with blessed feet, bringing good news of Sin and Death destroyed! O white-robed Angel, guide my timorous hand to write as on a lofty rock with iron pen the words of truth, that all who pass may read. Now Night, noon-tide of damned spirits, over the silent earth spreads her pavilion, while in dark council sat Philistia's lords; and where strength failed, black thoughts in ambush lay. There helmed youth and aged warriors in dust together lie, and Desolation spreads his wings over the land of Palestine: from side to side the land groans, her prowess lost, and seeks to hide her bruised head under the mists of night, breeding dark plots. For Dalila's fair arts have long been tried in vain; in vain she wept in many a treacherous tear. "Go on, fair traitress; do thy guileful work; ere once again the changing moon her circuit hath performed, thou shalt overcome, and conquer him by force unconquerable, and wrest his secret from him. Call thine alluring arts and honest-seeming brow, the holy kiss of love and the transparent tear; put on fair linen, that with the lily vies, purple and silver; neglect thy hair, to seem more lovely in thy loose attire; put on thy country's pride, deceit; and eyes of love decked in mild sorrow, and sell thy lord for gold." For now, upon her sumptuous couch, reclined, in gorgeous pride, she still entreats, and still she grasps his vigorous knees with her fair arms. "Thou lovest me not! thou'rt war, thou art not love! O foolish Dalila! O weak woman! it is death clothed in flesh thou lovest, and thou hast been encircled in his arms! Alas, my lord, what am I calling thee? Thou art my God![1] To thee I pour my tears for sacrifice morning and evening: my days are covered with sorrow! shut up, darkened: by night I am deceived! Who says that thou wast born of mortal kind? Destruction was thy father, a lioness suckled thee, thy young hands tore human limbs, and gorged human flesh! Come hither, Death; art thou not Samson's servant? 'Tis Dalila that calls; thy master's wife; no, stay, and let thy master do the deed: one blow of that strong arm would ease my pain; then I should lie at quiet and have rest. Pity forsook thee at thy birth! O Dagon furious, and all ye gods of Palestine, withdraw your hand! I am but a weak woman. Alas, I am wedded to your enemy! I will go mad, and tear my crisped hair; I'll run about, and pierce the ears o' th' gods! O Samson, hold me not; thou lovest me not! Look not upon me with those deathful eyes! Thou wouldst my death, and death approaches fast." Thus, in false tears, she bathed his feet, and thus she day by day oppressed his soul: he seemed a mountain, his brow among the clouds; she seemed a silver stream, his feet embracing. Dark thoughts rolled to and fro in his mind, like thunder clouds troubling the sky; his visage was troubled; his soul was distressed. "Though I should tell her all my heart, what can I fear? Though I should tell this secret of my birth, the utmost may be warded off as well when told as now." She saw him moved, and thus resumes her wiles: "Samson, I'm thine; do with me what thou wilt; my friends are enemies; my life is death; I am a traitor to my nation, and despised; my joy is given into the hands of him who hates me, using deceit to the wife of his bosom. Thrice hast thou mocked me and grieved my soul. Didst thou not tell me with green withes to bind thy nervous arms, and after that, when I had found thy falsehood, with new ropes to bind thee fast? I knew thou didst but mock me. Alas, when in thy sleep I bound thee with them to try thy truth, I cried, The Philistines be upon thee, Samson! then did suspicion wake thee; how didst thou rend the feeble ties! Thou fearest nought, what shouldst thou fear? Thy power is more than mortal, none can hurt thee; thy bones are brass, thy sinews are iron! Ten thousand spears are like the summer grass; an army of mighty men are as flocks in the valleys: what canst thou fear? I drink my tears like water; I live upon sorrow! O worse than wolves and tigers, what canst thou give when such a trifle is denied me? But, oh! at last thou mockest me, to shame my over-fond inquiry! Thou toldest me to weave thee to the beam by thy strong hair; I did even that to try thy truth: but when I cried, The Philistines be upon thee! then didst thou leave me to bewail that Samson loved me not." He sat, and inward grieved, he saw and loved the beauteous suppliant, nor could conceal aught that might appease her; then, leaning on her bosom, thus he spoke: "Hear, O Dalila! doubt no more of Samson's love; for that fair breast was made the ivory palace of my inmost heart, where it shall lie at rest; for sorrow is the lot of all of woman born: for care was I brought forth, and labour is my lot: nor matchless might, nor wisdom, nor every gift enjoyed, can from the heart of man hide sorrow. Twice was my birth foretold from heaven, and twice a sacred vow enjoined me that I should drink no wine, nor eat of any unclean thing, for holy unto Israel's God I am, a Nazarite even from my mother's womb. Twice was it told that it might not be broken: Grant me a son, kind Heaven, Manoa cried; but Heaven refused! Childless he mourned, but thought his God knew best. In solitude, though not obscure, in Israel he lived, till venerable age came on: his flocks increased, and plenty crowned his board: beloved, revered of man! But God hath other joys in store. Is burdened Israel his grief? The son of his old age shall set it free! The venerable sweetener of his life receives the promise first from Heaven. She saw the maidens play, and blessed their innocent mirth; she blessed each new-joined pair; but from her the long-wished deliverer shall spring. Pensive, alone she sat within the house, when busy day was fading, and calm evening, time for contemplation, rose from the forsaken east, and drew the curtains of heaven: pensive she sat, and thought on Israel's grief, and silent prayed to Israel's God; when lo! an angel from the fields of light entered the house: His form was manhood in the prime, and from his spacious brow shot terrors through the evening shade! But mild he hailed her—Hail, highly favoured! said he; for lo! thou shalt conceive, and bear a son, and Israel's strength shall be upon his shoulders, and he shall be called Israel's Deliverer. Now, therefore, drink no wine, and eat not any unclean thing, for he shall be a Nazarite to God.—Then, as a neighbour, when his evening tale is told, departs, his blessing leaving, so seemed he to depart: she wondered with exceeding joy, nor knew he was an angel. Manoa left his fields to sit in the house, and take his evening's rest from labour—the sweetest time that God has allotted mortal man. He sat, and heard with joy, and praised God, who Israel still doth keep. The time rolled on, and Israel groaned oppressed. The sword was bright, while the ploughshare rusted, till hope grew feeble, and was ready to give place to doubting; then prayed Manoa: O Lord, thy flock is scattered on the hills! The wolf teareth them: Oppression stretches his rod over our land, our country is ploughed with swords, and reaped in blood! The echoes of slaughter reach from hill to hill! Instead of peaceful pipe the shepherd bears a sword; the ox-goad is turned into a spear! O when shall our Deliverer come? The Philistine riots on our flocks, our vintage is gathered by bands of enemies! Stretch forth thy hand, and save. Thus prayed Manoa. The aged woman walked into the field, and lo! again the angel came! Clad as a traveller fresh risen on his journey. She ran and called her husband, who came and talked with him. O man of God, said he, thou comest from far! Let us detain thee while I make ready a kid, that thou mayest sit and eat, and tell us of thy name and warfare; that when thy sayings come to pass, we may honour thee. The angel answered, My name is Wonderful; inquire not after it, seeing it is a secret; but, if thou wilt, offer an offering unto the Lord."

CHISWICK PRESS:—PRINTED BY WHITTINGHAM AND WILKINS, TOOKS COURT, CHANCERY LANE.

1. Compare Tennyson's treatment of a similar subject in the Idyll of Vivien, where, after demanding of Merlin his secret, in order to undo him with it, she calls his love in question on his refusal, and then, changing her tactics:
"Call'd him her lord, her silver star of eve,
Her god, her Merlin."

Note from the Editor

Odin's Library Classics strives to bring you unedited and unabridged works of classical literature. As such this is the complete and unabridged version of the original English text. The English language has evolved since the writing and some of the words appear in their original form, or at least the most commonly used form at the time. This is done to protect the original intent of the author. If at any time you are unsure of the meaning of a word, please do your research on the etymology of that word. It is important to preserve the history of the English language.

Taylor Anderson

Printed in Great Britain
by Amazon

82201491R00037